when truth refreshes

DAILY REFLECTIONS
FROM SCRIPTURE
FOR THE EMOTIONS
THAT ACCOMPANY
THE LYME DISEASE JOURNEY

REBECCA VANDEMARK

WHEN TRUTH REFRESHES

dedication

for those who feel overwhelmed, lost, and alone by the emotions of the Lyme Journey

and for Ali who has consistently, graciously, and compassionately spoken gentle truth into the days of weeping

acknowledgments

It would be impossible to write this book without the consistent, supportive, and loving listening love and compassionately gentle truth that both my mom and dad have given every single day throughout all hours of the day and night. They have lived courageously in the dark, joyously in the hope of a better future, and most of all they have carried me each day, wiping away countless tears. They are *the* greatest gifts in this journey. Without them this book and its truths that I have learned would never have been discovered.

All scripture in this book has been noted or referenced in this book. There have been numerous versions used to help encourage the reader to look at a variety of different scriptural references in their journey. May you find peace, encouragement, and most of all gentle truth in hope in the living and active word of God.

content

a note from the author

Dear Fellow Lyme Warrior,

The book that you hold in your hand has been written from my heart. I found out I had Advanced Late Stage Lyme disease the day after my 33rd birthday. For the previous six years prior to that day I had experienced a myriad of intricate and confusing health symptoms that never made sense to any doctor. I had spent thousands of hours and dollars traveling across the United States talking and consulting with some of the best medical professionals in the country. Instead of finding answers I found these professionals stumped and mystified and I was eventually told by each of these doctors that either (a) this was "in my head", (b) I had a very "complex case" of Chronic Fatigue Syndrome (for which I had been diagnosed for) or (c) "stress was contributing to these issues". Finally, after seeing 273 doctors, seven years of searching, hundreds of invasive and painful tests, and thousands of prayers, I was correctly and accurately diagnosed with Advanced Late Stage Lyme disease.

To be frank, the journey through this disease has brought a myriad of emotions that have been more intense than anything else that I have ever experienced in my life. The range of emotions have shifted through loneliness, grief, fear, frustration, anger, hopefulness & hopelessness in addition to a myriad of other emotions discussed in this book.

I came across this quote by Paul David Tripp earlier this year and this past summer the Lord brought it to mind again and again, especially in finishing up the edits of this book: "Every day you preach to yourself a gospel of your loneliness, inability, and lack of resources or you faithfully preach to yourself the gospel of the Lord Jesus Christ."[i]

I need to do this. I needed this book. I still need this book. I need to be reminded of the truth of the gospel and the hope that comes from that. I need to preach to myself the gospel of Jesus Christ and the tender mercy that meets me in my emotional ups and downs, no matter the circumstances that Lyme throws at me.

My prayer with this little book is that it will encourage you, lead you to Scripture, remind you that you are not alone in this fight, and gently remind you that the God of hope and truth is very present and active in this often emotional journey. May the Lord bless you abundantly, dear friend, and give you strength for the journey before you and may we find everlasting hope in our ever present and faithful Savior.

Blessings, Rebecca

"Guide me in your truth and teach me, for you are God my Savior, and my hope is in you all day long."
-Psalm 25:5-

acceptance &contentment

definition (acceptance): "Belief in something; agreement."[ii]

definition (contentment): "To be free from care because of satisfaction with what is already one's own. The Hebrew means simply "to be pleased"."[iii]

"Build homes, and plan to stay. Plant gardens, and eat the food they produce."
-Jeremiah 29:5-

So many times in life it can be tempting to move or run away to a new place if our circumstances are not exactly how we envisioned them to be. If anything has the capacity to make us want to run away it is definitely in dealing with the journey of Lyme disease. There have been so many times that I have wanted to pack up, call it quits, and say "goodbye" to this stage of life. I have wept over it. I have dreamed of a different life. I have envisioned a beautiful and sick free existence. My heart wants to run far, far away from Lyme.

The problem is though that we really can't run away from our bodies can we? We can wish it so, but we can't completely run away. Some may think this would bring despair, but in reality, I am learning this brings a beautiful gift to our lives. We can learn an important lesson, the beautiful blessing and hope that comes with acceptance.

When life radically changed due to Lyme and I was

forced to move home to my parents house in a different state, I went from being an independent, social, active young woman, working in a job that I loved, living life with people, and enjoying being involved in my church and community to a woman that became primarily bedridden and alone.

The transition was incredibly difficult, and at the beginning there wasn't a day that didn't go by that was spent more in tears than in laughter. I deeply struggled with Scripture talking about contentment as I was unsure how this new life that I found myself in could be anything but sorrowful, stressful, and full of grief. I wept deeply and longed for the days when my life would return to "normal".

I was assured by many people that this season would be brief, but as I am approaching the five year mark of moving home, life in its beauty and horror has presented a different story. I longed to be in a different place- physically in my body and emotionally longing for the life that I had before.

But there is a beauty that I started to find in acceptance. A beauty that recognizes that life will always hold a mixture of sadness, wonderment, hope and joy, even when our journey with Lyme is complete.

My heart goes out to each of you struggling through tears just to read the first word on this page... acceptance. It can stir the best of our emotions, can't it? I weep with you if you are struggling, because my heart well understands where you are at. *Truly,* I do. I wish that I could sit down with you and just listen to your journey with Lyme and give you a gentle hug of encouragement. I can't begin to imagine how hard this road has been for you.

My precious mom has done this with me countless times in this journey. She has sat down, held my hand, and given me the space to cry and process the longing of wanting to be in a different season. Years ago my mom shared with me about a particularly difficult season in her own life when I was a young girl. Specifically she shared how difficult it was to live in one tiny house that I spent the first nine years of my life in. I was shocked to learn this because I had never suspected this at any point in my life. My mom had always been so joyful in that living arrangement, and as far as I had ever known she had not just survived, but thrived in that space.

One afternoon as I was weeping about issues with Lyme, my mom tenderly explained all of the things that had made that living arrangement a difficult place to live. She listed out numerous things and my mouth dropped open. I was stunned as I had never seen her be anything less than happy and content with her circumstances. I immediately asked her what her secret was.

Her reply was simple and yet so profound. She said, *"Jesus. Simply Jesus. I turned my eyes off of the circumstances that I couldn't change and loathed and back onto the One who loves me more than life. I resolved to find the joy there in that situation, no matter what the circumstances were to the contrary."* And then she continued and gently said,

"Rebecca, if you can't find contentment and happiness where you currently find yourself, you will never find it in a different set of circumstances."

My mom is my hero. She resolved to make her home where she was at and grew and flourished and found beauty in acceptance and most of all she learned to laugh at the things that would have made her cry. Throughout my life I have seen my mom consistently model this same trust and surrender to the Lord. Several decades after the little house season, I now again marvel at watching my mom resolve to find joy and contentment in her situations and surroundings. For the past four years she has tirelessly sacrificed any of her desires and dreams to help me get better. She retired early from a job she loved, has cooked countless of meals, taken me to thousands of doctors appointments (even ones across the country and out of the country), has sat in countless uncomfortable hospital chairs, wiped away daily tears, held my hair back when I have been sick time and time again, and has whispered constant hope and truth to me every single day. She has delighted in serving behind the scenes and has never once complained.

For the past several years we have lived more than 20 hours away from my parents house with my grandmother in her tiny home, so that I can receive treatments in my fight for my health. My parents have sacrificed deeply, giving up the ease of living in their own home and space and have never complained once. My parents love and focus on the Lord and not their circumstances has changed me in the best way possible. My mom continues to live out the principle from the tiny house season long ago... a life found in the joy and focus on the One that she loves the most.

Acceptance and contentment bring a beauty that could otherwise never be found.

Dear friends, no matter the painful and difficult circumstances with Lyme let us fight for the bravery to find joy and resolve right now. Let us fight the temptation to focus on the things that Lyme has taken away and find beauty in the gifts that we are surrounded with every day. Let us memorize and meditate on the gentle and loving truth of Scripture. Let us build our houses both physically and emotionally and plant gardens as we find acceptance and contentment in the One who loves us more than life.

And on the days where all we can do is cry, let us remember that the Lord is with us. We are not alone and we are not forgotten. For truly with acceptance and contentment there is great gain. (I Timothy 6:6)

"In acceptance lies peace."
-Amy Carmichael[iv]

acceptance &contentment prayer notes

_____

_____

_____

_____

_____

_____

_____

_____

_____

_____

_____

_____

_____

_____

anger & rage

definition (anger): "A strong feeling of displeasure and belligerence aroused by a wrong; an intense feeling."[v]

definition (rage): "A violent and uncontrolled anger..."[vi]

"For we are not fighting against flesh and blood, but against the rulers, against the authorities, against the cosmic powers over this present darkness, against the spiritual forces of evil..."
-Ephesians 6:12-

Two of the real emotions that many Lyme patients experience are the emotions of anger and rage. Lyme disease causes us to work through and grapple with these new and unique emotions in this journey.

Over the course of this journey I have met so many angry Lymies and I get it, I really do. The absolute anger at the length of time to get a diagnosis, anger at the way our bodies and our lives have been affected, anger at the medical community, anger at the lack of support and understanding, anger at people who abandon us in this journey, and anger at how our lives are nothing like we envisioned them to be. All of this has often brought me to my knees.

On the days that I am courageous enough I will also admit that I am angry at how Lyme disease is handled in our mainstream world. How could something that affects so many people not have a solution? How could the number of cases be increasing instead of diminishing? And if I am brutally honest, I am even angry at God for allowing this to happen and that this path is the one He has chosen to be the best one for my life.

Several years ago, during my first year into this journey and back at a time when I was severely affected by Lyme, I was unable to drive. One evening after another long day of pain and fruitless doctor appointments, I felt the anger starting to bubble up inside of me. All day long it had been a slow and burning anger that had been growing, and I justified it by the circumstances of the day.

The mail arrived and with it a letter from the state disability office which told me that my appeal for disability had been denied for the second time. As I sat holding the letter with tears streaming down my cheeks, I heard the noise of my car coming up to our home. My father had been using the car to run some necessary errands for me because I had felt too sick to do so. He stepped out of the car and started walking up to the front door.

As I sat on my bed looking out at the window I became incredibly angry. It seemed so unfair that just a few short months prior to this I had been able to work at a job that I loved, live in my own apartment, and drive whenever I wanted. For some reason at that exact moment my ever nauseous stomach decided that it wanted guacamole. For the next hour, I am embarrassed to say, I threw a toddler like temper tantrum that was less than lovely. There were tears and I even slammed my bedroom door as I insisted that I could drive to get the guacamole. Obviously this was impossible and eventually my kind-hearted father spent an hour in evening traffic retrieving the guacamole.

It didn't matter that there wasn't money to buy this or that it had been an exceptionally long day for both of my parents. The guacamole was all I wanted. But more than that, I felt anger as I wanted the freedom to be well enough to get in the car and go and do what I wanted to do when I wanted to do it.

Over the last several years there have been other "guacamole" longings and moments that have happened, although none have involved guacamole. In reality all of these situations revolve around anger stemming from frustration with dealing with this disease and the side effects it has left on my body.

The problem is that there is a reason why anger is considered one of the seven deadly sins. It has the potential to rob us of not only the joy of life, but of the potential of finding joy in the simplest of days and moments. Anger has the potential to steal the good even out of a very bad situation like dealing with Lyme disease.

Each of these "guacamole situations" (as I affectionately refer to them) has taught me that I don't want to be angry or let this potentially destructive emotion control my life. I have such little energy as it is, and the little that I do have I don't want to spend and waste on being angry at anything-especially at God.

In the moments where we feel most overwhelmed by anger let us ask the Lord to specifically help us use this emotion for His good purpose. Let us remember that our struggle is not against what we see, but against what we can't see. Let us pray and ask for help to use the energy of anger into bringing justice and hope into the world, specifically in the realm of Lyme disease and trust Him with this deep emotion. Most of all in the midst of the "guacamole situations" let us pray that God will guide our tender hearts with this very deep and real emotion.

"Bitterness is like Cancer. It eats upon the host. But anger is like fire. It burns it all clean."
-Maya Angelou-[vii]

anger & rage prayer notes

_____

_____

_____

_____

_____

_____

_____

_____

_____

_____

_____

_____

_____

apprehension

definition: "Anticipation of adversity or misfortune; suspicion or fear of future trouble or evil."[viii]

"She is clothed with strength and dignity, and she laughs without fear of the future."
-Proverbs 31:25-

It comes without fail. A wave of apprehension always sweeps over me as I anticipate an upcoming doctor's appointment or medical test. I have been in this "Lyme world" too long as I find myself thinking of the worst-case scenarios that could come from a new test or doctor's appointment. The apprehension pools in the depths of my stomach, and I find myself consumed with suspicion or fear of future trouble that could arise.

I was reading this past week in Luke and came across verse 26 in the 21st chapter which said, *"People will faint from terror, apprehensive of what is coming on the world…"* This verse stopped me short. This is exactly how I often am feeling: faint with terror and completely apprehensive of what is coming in my world. This journey with Lyme has the ability to wipe away all of the hopeful and good thoughts of the future. Instead of living carefree, I often find myself in bondage to thoughts of apprehension. Instead of laughter gracing our days, worry and tears become the norm.

All of the emotions of Lyme are difficult, but this one has the possibility to steal the peace from not only the present, but the future. A couple of weeks ago I found myself in this exact same position. After several weeks of starting to feel the best that I have felt in this Lyme journey I went in for a routine appointment expecting good news. Instead, less than an hour later I ended up discussing the real possibility of looking at Cancer, scheduling an unplanned surgery for less than three weeks later, and finding myself fighting countless tears dripping down my face. I felt that my shaky confidence in not fearing the future was immediately shattered and all I could see was death and apprehension.

This apprehension gripped me and I was apprehensive about the upcoming surgery. I found great comfort from the words of Isaiah, *"Tell those who are terrified, 'Be brave; don't be afraid. Your God will come... He will come and rescue you'."* (Isaiah 35:4)

Sweet friends, the next time that you feel that the emotion of apprehension threatens to overwhelm you, take time to meditate and lean on the truth of this verse. This verse is the beautiful "clothing" of strength and dignity that Proverbs 31:25 discusses.

As we clothe ourselves each day, reminding our apprehensive hearts of truth, we will see that we don't need to fear what the future holds. We can face each day laughing without apprehension of the future.

"They do not fear bad news; they confidently trust the Lord to care for them."
-Psalm of David, Psalm 112:7 [ix]

apprehension prayer notes

_____

_____

_____

_____

_____

_____

_____

_____

_____

_____

_____

_____

_____

anticipation

*definition: "A prior action that takes into account or forestalls
a later action; the act of looking forward; visualization of a
future event or state."*[x]

"But as for me, I will watch expectantly for the Lord;
I will wait for the God of my salvation. My God will
hear me."
-Micah 7:7-

I have always thought of anticipation as the expectant
waiting to be healed of Lyme disease and to be
"moving on" into a different season filled with health
and joy. I was surprised as I considered the true
definition of anticipation to be what is stated above.
The true definition of the word actually takes into
account the fact that a prior action is being taken
while looking forward. In other words, I see clearly
that we are not anticipating fruitlessly as we continue
to work on our treatment protocols, but instead, that
we are actually working towards our goal as we
anticipate life in the future.

This past summer I had the opportunity to attend a
dear friends wedding out of state. It was the first time
that I had really traveled by myself to attend a
wedding in the years since I had become progressively
worse with Lyme. There had been so many times
where I had had to say "no" to special events that
being able to go to this wedding was a dream. I
carefully planned, packed, and for months anticipated
how wonderful each moment was going to be.

Unfortunately, the reality turned out to be a bit
different than my tender heart had hoped and
dreamed. It was a lovely time, but not as much as my
mind had anticipated it to be. I walked away from it a
bit disillusioned and wondered if I was creating in my
mind how wonderful life would be without Lyme. I
realized that I was.

Look, life without Lyme will be wonderful, and I am
working as hard as I can to get there. This experience
tenderly taught me that beyond anticipating things
that happen here on earth, my expectations should be
for heaven. This is where my anticipation could never
could never disappoint me. There will be absolutely
no pain, no sickness, and definitely no Lyme disease.
Can you imagine?? I am humbled and in awe of the
concept. It is beyond my mind.

As we continue to work hard to fight this disease let
us anticipate the beauty that will meet us in the good
and bad days ahead, but even more so the perfect
beauty that will meet us in heaven. Let us be amazed
at the idea that all of our anticipation could never
even come close to how wonderful heaven will be.
Let us run this race well, friends, and wait expectantly
for the Lord who is the God of our salvation.

"Strength for today and bright hope for tomorrow..."
-Thomas Chisholm[xi]

anticipation prayer notes

_____

_____

_____

_____

_____

_____

_____

_____

_____

_____

_____

_____

_____

_____

boredom

definition: "To weary by dullness, tedious repletion…"[xii]

"Whatever presents itself for you to do, do it with all
of your might…"
-Ecclesiastes 9:10, *GOD'S WORD Translation*-

One of the emotions that easily accompanies the
Lyme disease journey is dealing with boredom. By
definition, boredom means to weary by dullness and
to be honest- nothing has the capacity to bring us to
boredom more than the tedious requirements to beat
this disease. Working day after day and hour after
hour to do different treatments, taking our medicines,
taking supplements, completing doctors instructions,
going to various doctors' appointments, etc. There is
so much to do and yet there is a boredom that can
come from the monotony day after day and there also
can be a danger in this emotion.

Several years ago ESPN reported the tragic story of
22 year old Christopher Lane who was an Australian
baseball player living in Oklahoma. One day, while he
was running he was shot and killed by 3 teens. When
the teens were later arrested and asked the reason that
they shot Christopher in the back they replied that
they had been "bored".[xiii] Their response illuminates
Martyn Lloyd James' quote, *"Sin is always, in some sense
a life of boredom."*[xiv]

Following this statement through to the concept and
reality of hell, we are struck by the reality that hell at

its most basic existence is boring. It is the most boring place and existence of all because there is nothing new there. There is no new life. There is no new joy to be found. There is no purpose to be found there. There is only pain and suffering repeated again and again and again for all eternity with no opportunity for relief. There is nothing but boredom of pain and suffering, because Jesus is not present there and with Jesus there is no hope.

And sometimes… if we are honest, this disease has the propensity to make us feel that we are in hell. We are living our worst nightmare day after day after day with no relief.

But hope in the Lord is anything but boring despite the circumstances that we find ourselves in with this disease. We can be assured that serving the Lord even in this seemingly repetitive and tedious job in front of us has meaning. Resting and relying on this brings a truth to our lives, but most importantly it brings a reason out of boredom. Even in the midst of our boring daily routine we can find purpose and lots of joy and meaning. No matter what- we can find joy, meaning, and purpose in knowing that boredom is never what fills our days. We are not in hell, even though we may feel a taste of it. Instead we are gently and graciously and tenderly carried in hope. And this alone brings our days full of love and purpose, with no boredom.

"A Christian is never bored or sad. Rather, the one who loves Christ is full of joy and radiates joy."
-Pope Francis-[xv]

boredom prayer notes

_____

_____

_____

_____

_____

_____

_____

_____

_____

_____

_____

_____

_____

_____

_____

courage

definition: "Mental or moral strength to venture, persevere, and withstand danger, fear, or difficulty."[xvi]

"So be strong and courageous, all you who put your
hope in the LORD!"
-Psalm 31:24-

If there is one thing that we need for the Lyme
disease journey it is courage. We need to have the
mental and moral strength to venture into this
disease, persevering without fear. We need it.
Scripture has numerous verses to push us in that
direction, and yet often times courage can wax and
wane in the length of this journey.

For the past several years I have joined in on the
"pick a word for the year" train that you often see on
social media. For the first couple of years I chose
words that encompassed the theme of courage. One
year I chose valor and another year I chose mettle.
Both words in different ways share a recurring theme
that I needed. The concept of courageously stepping
forward to do all I could to beat Lyme and its co-
infections.

I find great comfort and encouragement to press on
in courage as Scripture is filled with verses that speak
to this important topic. And we need those verses
don't we? I know I do. I need to be reminded that I
am not alone in this journey. I need to be reminded
that I am not having courage whimsically because the

God of the universe is by my side.

One of my favorite passages comes from
Deuteronomy 31. It states:

*"Be strong and courageous. Do not be afraid or terrified because
of them, for the LORD your God goes with you; He will never
leave you nor forsake you. Then Moses summoned Joshua and
said to him in the presence of all Israel, 'Be strong and
courageous...The Lord himself goes before you and will be with
you; He will never leave you nor forsake you. Do not be afraid;
do not be discouraged'."[xvii]*

Be strong friends. Be courageous. Let us find our
courage in knowing the Lord fully. This battle for our
health is so incredibly difficult and demanding and it
calls for courage from the deepest parts of our souls.
But just like Moses promised Joshua, we can find the
same promise of truth. The Lord will go before us
and He will be with us. He will never leave us or
forsake us. We are not alone. We are not in this Lyme
journey alone. Don't be afraid, have courage.

*"If your God's child, you can live with hope and courage
because your Heavenly Father knows exactly what you need. If
you're God's child, you can live with hope and courage because
your Savior rules over all things for His glory and your good. If
you're God's child, you can live with hope and courage because
you are the object of forgiving, empowering grace."*
-Paul Tripp-[xviii]

courage prayer notes

_____

_____

_____

_____

_____

_____

_____

_____

_____

_____

_____

_____

_____

_____

despair

definition: "To lose, give up, or be without hope."[xix]

"Nevertheless, that time of darkness and despair will
not go on forever."
-Isaiah 9:1-

Throughout this journey there have been times where
I have felt utter despair. It can be so hard day after
day to hold on to hope when you don't see
improvements and you don't see the changes that you
are longing for. Your heart longs for it and your mind
wills for change, but despair creeps in and sometimes
can take a hold in the deepest parts of our souls.

Sometimes we set our hopes on improving with the
latest idea or latest treatment option only to be
severely disappointed into despair. Other times we
continue day after day plugging away at our treatment
protocol with no improvement. When we see how
ideas don't help, or we have tried something that has
helped another, but doesn't help us we can start to
lose the tenuous hope that we struggle to hold on to
day after day, week after week, and month after
month.

I recently was listening to an older sermon from one
of my favorite pastors on the life of Paul and the
theme of not losing heart[xx]. At the beginning of the
sermon the pastor went through just a few of the
things that Paul endured throughout his lifetime
including being thrown in jail, enduring beatings and

stoning, enduring friendly fire from Christians, losing friends, being forced to leave places and positions he loved, enduring imprisonments and afflictions and the list goes on and on and on. Having it presented like this made me truly pause, especially when Paul admits that he himself, the great and wonderful apostle of the Bible, despaired of life. *"We do not want you to be uninformed, brothers and sisters, about the troubles we experienced in the province of Asia. We were under great pressure, far beyond our ability to endure, so that we despaired of life itself."* (2 Corinthians 1:8)

What kept Paul going? What kept him for losing heart? Paul had learned the great lesson that his life was nothing apart from Jesus. No matter what he endured the adequacy of God's grace met him each and every single day.

The verse from Isaiah 9 has been a great comfort to me in this very long journey. I have always found it to be so hopeful, especially considering how the ending of Isaiah 8 talks about being trapped in darkness. *"Distressed and hungry, they will roam through the land; when they are famished, they will become enraged and, looking upward, will curse their king and their God. Then they will look toward the earth and see only distress and darkness and fearful gloom, and they will be thrust into utter darkness."* (Isaiah 8:21-22) Often in the journey with Lyme it is easy to feel and experience despair, and it feels like we are just roaming aimlessly throughout the land. As we look around we often only see distress and darkness and fearful gloom. But the beautiful thing is that Isaiah 9 promises that the time of darkness and despair will not go on forever. Our despair and our darkness with walking through this disease will not last forever. Just like God met Paul throughout his countless troubles, God will meet us in our despair. Friends, do not lose hope. *"Suffering is not an accident, it is a divine appointment."*[xxi]

When it is too difficult to deal with the overwhelming nature of this disease and the very long journey, then let us take things one minute at a time, one slow hour at a time, and one very slow day at a time trusting that the time of darkness and despair will not last forever.

"We must never despair; our situation has been compromising before, and it has changed for the better; so I trust it will again."
-President George Washington[xxii]

despair prayer notes

_____

_____

_____

_____

_____

_____

_____

_____

_____

_____

_____

_____

_____

_____

_____

_____

disgust

definition: "To provoke to loathing, repugnance, or aversion; be offensive to; to cause (one) to lose an interest or intention."[xxiii]

"I look at the faithless with disgust, because they do
not keep your commands."
-Psalm 119:158-

When I consider the feeling of disgust in this journey there have been several key points where this type of feeling has arisen. To be frank, it has mostly revolved around three different things: (1) the medical community that continues to debate the existence of Lyme disease, (2) the disease itself which seems to continue to attack thousands of victims each year, (3) the lack of appropriate medical knowledge about how to prevent against the spread of Lyme disease and, finally (4) a lack of a cure.

I won't bore you with going into any of these four items as I am confident that any Lyme patient has felt disgust at one or more of these issues over the course of this Lyme journey. What I do want to move to is what we do with that disgust that we feel.

What do we do with the feelings of disgust that threaten to overwhelm us when we encounter one of the above things? What do we do when we have doctors that we are forced to interact with that won't acknowledge the realities of Lyme disease? What do we do when the disease itself continues to push and press into our bodies in new ways? What do we do when we hear of friends who find bulls eye rashes on their skin and they tell us that their doctors tell them that they don't need medicine? What do we do when…the list goes on and on.

It is in these moments that I realize that this feeling of disgust has the potential and amazing possibility to change the world if I let it. Instead of wasting time being upset and disgusted I can use this energy to propel me into asking the Lord how I can be faithful with this time and knowledge that He has given me. The verse at the beginning of this chapter from Psalm 119:158 may appear like a strange choice, but as I have been thinking about it I don't want to be a faithless one. I want to be faithful with the knowledge of Lyme and faithful to the Lord with how I can use this knowledge to change the world.

Maybe this means spending time writing informative letters to doctors who don't understand the complexity of Lyme disease. Maybe this means taking the time to educate friends who get a bulls eye rash. Maybe this means having the courage to give myself a little extra grace when Lyme creates new issues. Whatever it is I am determined to place this feeling before the Lord and to trust that He can use everything for our good, even the emotions of feeling disgust.

"Disgust and resolve are two of the greatest emotions that lead to change."
-Jim Rohn[xxiv]

disgust prayer notes

_____

_____

_____

_____

_____

_____

_____

_____

_____

_____

_____

_____

_____

_____

_____

_____

distraction

definition: "The act of distracting or the state of being distracted; something that distracts."[xxv]

"They went to …Gethsemane, and Jesus said, 'Sit here while I go and pray'...Then He returned and found the disciples asleep. He said to Peter, 'Simon, are you asleep? Couldn't you watch with me even one hour? Keep watch and pray so that you will not give in to temptation. For the spirit is willing, but the body is weak'. Then Jesus left them again and prayed the same prayer as before. When he returned to them again, he found them sleeping, for they couldn't keep their eyes open. And they didn't know what to say."
-Mark 14:32, 37-40-

Choosing what we do with our time is one of the most important decisions that we make every day. I am sure that we all have heard quotes, sayings, etc. based on how important it is to make wise decisions with our time, as we never know what the future holds. I completely agree with that, but even more so I have been contemplating how to spend time in this season of life, in this very hard and difficult season as I fight Lyme disease.

In the very difficult and dramatic seasons of life, like in the midst of this Lyme fight, it can be easy to whittle away time with things that aren't that important. Perhaps even more than when things are going "good" in life, there is a temptation to "veg out" and to be distracted. I have seen and been tempted myself on really difficult health days to "veg out" and to spend time on social media, being distracted and just scroll through countless pictures of people's lives who seem "perfect". But honestly I am learning a really hard, but important lesson in this season. It is the lesson of choosing to not be distracted, but to be wise with my time no matter the season.

It occurred to me through reading the verses in Mark chapter 14 a couple of important things. First, our enemy is alive and at work in the world and we live and operate not only in the things we see, but in the unseen. One of the ways that we are easily distracted by accomplishing things that God would have us do is through "tiredness" and in "vegging out". Second, I definitely think that being tired and needing rest are real things! Jesus talks in Scripture about resting in Him. Fighting Lyme disease and its co-infections often leaves me physically exhausted, and yet I am challenged to admit that I seem to be able to find time to idly spend on social media, but sometimes struggle to put energy into memorizing Scripture. I am humbled to acknowledge that I might spend hours watching TV to help me on difficult pain days as I am forced to lay in bed, but struggle to read and meditate on Scripture. And the list goes on and on.

Friends, going through Lyme disease is not an excuse for us to be given a "free pass" with our time. Instead, we are challenged to acknowledge that there are days that are too dark for those of us that are suffering to see the light, yet God is light. He brightens the path before us and before each step that we take. One of my favorite verses from this is from Isaiah 60:1-2, *"Arise, shine, for your light has come, and the glory of the LORD rises upon you. See, darkness covers the earth and thick darkness is over the peoples, but the LORD rises upon you and His glory appears over you."*

There are experiences and times that are so extreme that they crush us and we struggle to have hope. But, dear friends, let us find our hope not in "vegging out", but instead in the Hope that will *not* disappoint us. *"I pray that God, the source of hope, will fill you completely with joy and peace because you trust in him. Then you will overflow with confident hope through the power of the Holy Spirit."* (Romans 15:13) There are days where the valleys that we are in seem so deep and difficult that it seems that we will never find relief. But it is in those valleys that the Lord meets us in new ways that we never would have experienced had we not been in them. In those valleys we see the love of the Lord in new angles and see him at work in new ways then we ever thought possible. *"I will lead the blind by ways they have not known, along unfamiliar paths I will guide them; I will turn the darkness into light before them."* (Isaiah 42:16)

I urge you sweet friends to not ignore or try to distract and pass by the hard seasons by "vegging out", instead let us dig into Scripture and press on to know our Savior in new ways. Let the truth of His word fill our hearts as we wait on Him to answer us in our struggles. May His hope fill our hurting hearts like nothing else can because He will answer us when we are in distress. *"Oh, that we might know the LORD! Let us press on to know him. He will respond to us as surely as the arrival of dawn or the coming of rains in early spring."* (Hosea 6:3)

"If destruction fails to entangle us, distraction will do its best."
-Beth Moore-[xxvi]

distraction prayer notes

_____

_____

_____

_____

_____

_____

_____

_____

_____

_____

_____

_____

_____

_____

fear

definition: "A distressing emotion aroused by impending danger, evil, pain, etc., whether the threat is real or imagined."[xxvii]

"I stretch myself out. I sleep. Then I'm up again-
rested, tall and steady, Fearless before the enemy
mobs coming at me from all sides."
-Psalm 3:5-6, THE MESSAGE-

One of my greatest enemies in this journey is my
struggle with the feelings of fear. My fear ranges from
fears dealing with Lyme disease and its co-infections
to what could possibly go wrong next. Sometimes
those fears revolve around what could come next
with this disease and sometimes I feel like I am
holding my breath every time the phone rings,
expecting bad news.

Many times though my fears revolve directly around
Lyme and all that it entails. Questions like, "What if
my symptoms grow worse instead of better?" or
"What if I never beat this disease and spend the rest
of my life in bed?" or "What if the pain never
subsides?" or "What if something happens to my
caregivers?" and so many other "what if?" questions
threaten to overwhelm my mind.

I don't have perfect answers for these tough
questions. Instead, the Lord bids us to trust Him with
each of our days and moments. One of my favorite
verses on the topic of fear comes from Psalm 3:8. It
says, *"From the Lord comes deliverance. May your blessing be*

on your people." I definitely need the deliverance from the darkness of fear.

I once heard a pastor say that there are 365 Bible verses on the topic of being afraid and fear. Isn't that amazing? God has the littlest detail under control and lovingly shows us this with this topic of fear.

Fear in this disease is normal, but living in fear and being fearful do not have to rob us of the beauty of trusting the Lord. Since this is something that I struggle with greatly, I have been working on memorizing some of those 365 verses. My goal is to memorize them all so that I have truth for each day of the year of my life.

As we mediate and memorize Scripture, the Lord will remove and make the darkness of fear disappear in the light of His glory. *"You light a lamp for me. The LORD, my God, lights up my darkness."* (Psalm 18:28)

Today as we face fears of the future, of this disease, and fear of bad news let us remember that God is with us and has told us not to fear. We can, with His help, be fearless before our enemy of Lyme that comes at us from all sides. We can say confidently with the Psalmist, *"When I am afraid, I put my trust in you."* (Psalm 56:3)

"Every fear has no place at the sound of your great name…"
-Natalie Grant-[xxviii]

fear prayer notes

_____

_____

_____

_____

_____

_____

_____

_____

_____

_____

_____

_____

_____

_____

frustration

definition: "A feeling of being upset or annoyed as a result of being unable to change or achieve something; the prevention of the progress, success, or fulfillment of something."[xxix]

"So let's not get tired of doing what is good. At just the right time we will reap a harvest of blessing if we don't give up."
-Galatians 6:9-

This past summer my frustration level reached its fragile limit. Of course over the length of my journey with Lyme, I have felt frustrated at different times. I would work through these seasons of frustration and try to move forward forgetting these difficult times.

But this summer was different. I had a plan that included seeing tons of improvement by the fall only to be sidelined and not be able to do even a ¼ of the treatment that had been planned. Instead of getting better things got progressively worse. An alternative treatment intended to help heal set me back struggling with old symptoms that I hadn't experienced in years.

Just as I started to recover I found a bulls eye rash and needed to go on antibiotic treatment that irritated my fragile GI system. Five days later pain in my tooth started to escalate and a trip to the dentist revealed that I had an infection and needed a different oral antibiotic that caused additional GI issues and pain.

On top of all of these things it became apparent that

another med was causing more issues. Day after day and week after week things multiplied and grew. Aggressive treatment for Lyme was put on hold and with it my dreams of a productive summer with treatment shattered.

At first I tried to remain patient, taking one thing at a time, but below the surface my frustration level grew and grew. I was often in tears and no one seemed to know what to say. My poor loved ones were often left heartbroken at the lack of closure of this extremely frustrating season. I was frustrated at not only the inability to move forward, but mostly my inability to change any of the circumstances of my situation.

The verse from Galatians really spoke to my heart as it encouraged me to continue moving forward in the promise of blessings that would come if I did not give up. I realized that my feelings of frustration were justified, but it wasn't helping me in my desire to get better. I slowly started to realize that while I might not be able to change the course of events, the one thing that I could change was how I was going to spend my limited energy. I didn't want to put it towards frustration.

Finally, on a quiet Sunday morning I cried and sobbed one more time over frustration and the summer months of plans gone differently, and laid it finally in the hands of the One who loves me most.

I may not understand the delays or the long detours that come with this journey, but I do know that as we continue to press forward the Lord promises to bring a harvest of blessing. Don't give up friends. Our blessings are coming just beyond the long road of frustration.

"Sometimes the strongest people in the morning are the people who cried all night."
*-Unknown-*xxx

frustration prayer notes

_____

_____

_____

_____

_____

_____

_____

_____

_____

_____

_____

_____

_____

grief

definition: "The normal process of reacting to a loss. The loss may be physical (such as death), social (such as divorce), or occupational (such as a job)."[xxxi]

"Surely He has borne our griefs…"
-Isaiah 53:4-

In walking the road of Lyme disease, I believe we are automatically confronted with the emotion of grief.

Grief over the loss of easy physical abilities.

Grief over the social changes that occur.

Grief over relationship changes.

Grief over occupational changes.

Grief over huge things.

Grief over a hundred little things.

In my wildest dreams I could never have imagined that this would be the life that I would have at my age or any age if I am honest. I don't think any of us in life picture fighting a serious and deadly illness as part of our life's dreams or hopes. We never could imagine the ups and downs, the twists and turns, the long delays and detours, and all of the other ins and outs of Lyme disease.

I grieve for the way that Lyme has affected my body.
I grieve for the body that I don't recognize in the
mirror anymore. Lyme has changed it, and when I see
my dark eye shadows, the weight change, the lack of
sparkle in my eyes, the loss of hair, the skin rashes,
and the numerous other ways that Lyme has affected
me, I grieve for the body I used to have and the one I
long to have.

But even more than my physical changes I grieve for
the girl that lost who she was emotionally. Instead of
the easy-going girl whose social life was full of activity
and life, I now find myself a person who thinks
deeply over every single choice. Will "this or that" set
me back? Will eating "this or that" cause a reaction?
Will attending "this or that" social gathering cause me
to crash? The questions overcrowd my mind, and the
typical easy-going girl that I once knew is swallowed
up into a shell of who she was.

I was talking with a good friend recently and I said to
her, *"I am in a season of grief"*. Grief over everything I
have listed and grief that is too deep for words. Grief
over things that only those in the journey can
understand.

In the darkness I have been finding great hope in the
Scripture promise that states: *"But the needy will not be
ignored forever; the hopes of the poor will not always be
crushed."* (Psalm 9:18). This verse has spoken to my
hurting heart as I sometimes feel that I am being
ignored in my grief, and yet feel encouraged that this
verse promises that our hopes will not always be
crushed.

Friends, when we feel consumed by grief, let us remember this gentle hope and grace of this verse and timidly and tearfully rest in the peace of knowing that my times are in God's hands. *"But I am trusting you, O LORD, saying, 'You are my God!' My future is in your hands..."*(Psalm 31:14-15)

"Occasionally weep deeply over the life you hoped would be. Grieve the losses. Then wash your face. Trust God. And embrace the life you have."
-John Piper[xxxii]

grief prayer notes

_____

_____

_____

_____

_____

_____

_____

_____

_____

_____

_____

_____

_____

_____

guilt

definition: "A feeling of culpability, especially for imagined offenses."[xxxiii]

"Yet if anyone suffers as a Christian, let him not be
ashamed, but let him glorify God in that name."
-I Peter 4:16-

One of the real emotions that I experience in this
Lyme journey is the emotion of guilt. Guilt over how
little I am able to do compared to my life before
Lyme. Guilt over the constant story of pain and
sickness that surrounds everyone's life who loves me.
Guilt that people have dipped into their savings, their
retirement funds, their checking accounts, and more
to help me pay for treatment. Guilt that I am not
getting better faster. Guilt that everyone who loves
me looks so exhausted. Guilt that I ask friends for the
same repeated prayer request again and again and
again. Guilt over several thousand big things in life,
and guilt over a million little ones.

What do we do with this emotion of guilt that
threatens to overwhelm us? When guilt comes it can
feel like a tidal wave that crushes me. I sometimes feel
like I have been lost up in it and don't know how to
get over it.

I have found the best way to handle the different
facets of guilt in this journey is to take one day at a
time and to face the feelings head on. Instead of
spending hours of time scrolling through social media

and comparing my life to the journey that God has others on, I instead focus on where He has called me. Right now, no matter my feelings I am here. I am in the midst of this Lyme journey. I am in the midst of the fight before me. If I truly believe that God is in control than I have to trust that He will see to all of the little things that make me feel guilty. Just like He will take care of me each and every day, He will see to the needs of those who are walking this journey with me.

In doing this, I start to relinquish and realize that I have an opportunity to use these times of guilty feelings to bring unique glory to the Lord. This story isn't about me. It is all about Him. I don't need to feel guilty, because I am not ashamed of the path that the Lord has set before me.

Today, place the feeling of guilt in the Hands of the One who loves us most. Just think, friend, where you feel guilty in this story may be the one thing that God will use to bring others to Him.

Throw off the guilt, friends. Run this race with gracious knowledge that God has set the path before us. *"Therefore, since we are surrounded by such a huge crowd of witnesses to the life of faith, let us strip off every weight that slows us down… and let us run with endurance the race God has set before us."* (Hebrews 12:1)

"Guilt is a rope that wears thin."
-Ayn Rand[xxxiv]

guilt prayer notes

_____

_____

_____

_____

_____

_____

_____

_____

_____

_____

_____

_____

_____

_____

_____

hope

definition: "The feeling that what is wanted can be had or that events will turn out for the best."[xxxv]

"O Israel, hope in the Lord; for with the Lord there is unfailing love. His redemption overflows."
-Psalm 130:7-

In this journey with Lyme, the one emotion that can fluctuate the most is hope. Some days it can seem that we have a feeling that this Lyme disease will end and that eventually we will regain the lives of health that we desperately long for. The next day we can be hit with a herx so difficult that we can barely breathe, testing our hopeful feelings.

I often find myself begging the Lord to have mercy on my fragile body and spirit. I feel that I come to a shaky acceptance of hope only to have one little thing throw everything off reminding me that this battle seems hopeless.

Each night as I lay down, I weep with longing for this journey to be over and beg the Lord for healing. *"I am worn out from groaning Lord. All night long I flood my bed with weeping and drench my couch with tears. My eyes grow weak with sorrow..."* (Psalm 6: 6-7) I look at this battle with this awful disease and *"my soul is in deep anguish. How long, LORD, how long?".*(Psalm 6:3) My heart cries in the depths of the night and the darkness of the soul.

The words of the Psalmist gently strengthen my heart and give me courage for the length of this journey: *"So be strong and courageous, all you who put your hope in the LORD!"* (Psalm 31:24)

We may feel that our hope is waning as the days grow long with suffering. It is during those times that I find myself questioning what exactly I have placed my hope in. If it is on healing, that is not enough. My hope must be placed on the Lord completely and solely. As I put my hope in the Lord I know that I will find unfailing love and hope. *"We wait in hope for the LORD; He is our help and our shield. In Him our hearts rejoice, for we trust in His holy name. Let your unfailing love surround us, LORD, for our hope is in you alone."* (Psalm 33:20-22) Our hope is secure in God and we trust in His unfailing love.

So, dear friends, on the days where the path seems to hold no hope, remember that our God is our ultimate hope.

"Biblical hope is the confident expectation that God is willing and able to fulfill the promises He has made to those who trust Him."
-Lee Strobel-[xxxvi]

hope prayer notes

_____

_____

_____

_____

_____

_____

_____

_____

_____

_____

_____

_____

_____

hopelessness

*definition: "Providing no hope; beyond optimism or hope;
desperate, without hope, despairing."*[xxxvii]

"The Lord is near to those who are discouraged; he
saves those who have lost all hope."
-Psalm 34:18-

When I found out I had Advanced Late Stage Lyme
disease the day after my 33rd birthday, I broke down
and wept. Then I proceeded to yell at my precious
mom, becoming hysterical in my grief, and cried more
tears than I had in the previous six years in a matter
of eight hours.

My response (obviously) wasn't one of joy at finding a
correct diagnosis, or relief that answers were finally
given, or even triumph in knowing that I had
persevered through hundreds of doctors telling me
that "nothing was wrong". Instead, it was one of deep
hopelessness for I was sure that if the answer to
finding a diagnosis had been so difficult, than beating
this misunderstood disease would be impossible. I
had also read the horror stories online and each one
offered only hopelessness at what I now faced.

At the beginning I felt hopeless, but over the years I
found incredible hope and encouragement in reading
and memorizing the Psalms. I have always loved the
Psalms, but none so much as since this journey began.
As I approach another anniversary of when this
season began and everything was shattered, I look

back on the now tattered pages of the book of Psalms in my Bible with a smile. These 150 chapters have provided much comfort and hope, especially on days where I felt that even crying was too painful.

In the middle of the night 10 hours after I was given my diagnosis I read Psalm 10:17 and it has been the "battle cry" of my heart since that grief-stricken and hopeless day.

Dear friends, you may be feeling like I did at the beginning of this journey. You may feel hopeless at what is in front of you having just received an official diagnosis. You may be feeling hopeless because money has dried up, and there is no possible way to pay for treatment. You may be feeling hopeless at the lack of improvement that intense treatment has brought to you. You may be feeling hopeless because a medical professional is saying that there is absolutely no hope for your case.

Whatever the reason is that you feel hopeless, I want to assure you that your life and your story is anything but hopeless. Rest in His truth and promises today friends. You are not alone. Your story is not finished. Your story will end with hope. *"LORD, you know the hopes of the helpless. Surely you will hear their cries and comfort them."* (Psalm 10:17)

"Is your hope an anchor for your soul? Has your wishful hope been converted at the foot of the cross to true hope? Job's well-tested hope was enlivened by true faith in God:

"Though He slay me, yet I will hope in Him."

That's quite a lot different from merely hoping for the most comfortable outcome! Could it be that our suffering... provides us with raw material for true hope? Hosea thought so. Speaking for God, he wrote,

"I will make the Valley of Anchor [which means "trouble"] a door of hope" (Hosea 2:15).

I find it interesting that achor and anchor are so similar in spelling...Today, twenty-seven centuries after Hosea prophesied those words of hope, we can look at them with the aid of the Light that has come into this world. Whatever our lot, He can do it. He can walk into our valley of trouble and convert all our false hope to true hope, where we can be anchored securely."
-Elisabeth Elliot-xxxviii

hopelessness prayer notes

_____

_____

_____

_____

_____

_____

_____

_____

_____

_____

_____

_____

_____

_____

_____

jealousy

*definition: "Feeling resentment because of another's success, advantage, etc."*xxxix

"They seem to live such painless lives; their bodies are
so healthy and strong."
-Psalm 73:4-

At some point or another in this Lyme disease
journey, we all struggle with the green-eyed monster.
When I read Psalm 73:4, I find great comfort in
knowing that I am not the only one who has struggled
with these feelings of jealousy that many people have
no health struggles. I have found that it can be hard
to relate in some ways, and if I am honest, it is
because I feel that many people's non-health related
struggles are incredibly easy.

As I struggle on some days to even sit up in bed or to
even have the strength to get out of bed, I do envy
those around me who do not have to deal with any
health issues. From my vantage point it seems like the
psalmist so adequately stated that they have no
challenges. As I watch them go "blithely" on their
way or listen to the complaints of those who have no
health concerns, I envy the fact that they can have the
struggles that they are talking about.

Complaining about their jobs? I so wish that I had a
job to complain about! Complaining about their
friends choosing the same restaurant over and over
again? I so wish that I had the strength to go out to

eat. Complaining about friends in general? I miss the constant phone calls and social activities that came with a normal and healthy social life. Complaining about their health insurance going up? I wish that health insurance aside from the mounting doctors' bills was my only concern.

If I let it, the list could go on and on with no end. I envy at the end of the day that it appears that *"they are free from common human burdens"* (Psalm 73:5). I envy that *"they are not plagued by human ills".* (Psalm 73:5).

But mostly, if I am courageous enough to admit it, I am envious that my story, the one that the Lord is writing for me, includes Lyme disease. It really has nothing to do with the fact that others don't have health concerns or a list of diagnosis's a page long. Of course, I wouldn't want anyone to deal with Lyme or the pain and sickness that we deal with. I am envious, and I am stopped short that I have to face the fact that my story includes the broken part of sin and illness. That is what I am really struggling with in regards to jealousy.

But when I live there – when I live comparing or having a quick answer in my head about what I wish I could complain about, I miss the abundant blessings that God has given me.

I am not just this disease that I am fighting. I am not just a patient.

When I get caught up in this self-pity envy, I miss out on the abundant blessings that the Lord has bestowed upon me. *"Yes, the LORD pours down His blessings. Our land will yield its bountiful harvest."* (Psalm 85:12) Let us pray that the Lord would help us see clearly the abundant blessings that we have been given and ask for help not to be caught up in envy that only leads to destruction. *"A peaceful heart leads to a healthy body; jealousy is like Cancer to the bones."* (Proverbs 14:30)

"If we let it, our jealousy may end up being one of the greatest teachers in our lives to lead us back to the beauty and the generosity of the Lord."
-Rebecca VanDeMark-[xl]

jealousy prayer notes

_____

_____

_____

_____

_____

_____

_____

_____

_____

_____

_____

_____

_____

_____

_____

_____

joy

definition: "The emotion evoked by well-being, success, or good fortune or by the prospect of possessing what one desires; a source of cause of delight."[xli]

"You reveal the path of life to me; in Your presence is abundant joy…"
-Psalm 16:11-

Joy, as this journey with Lyme disease has taught me, goes beyond the concept of happiness and laughter. Joy reveals my deepest character in showing my utter trust or lack of trust in the Lord in spite of the circumstances that I am facing.

Each day we have the opportunity to learn from the truth of Psalm 16:11 that in His presence we find our abundant joy. Not in how the day is going or what side effects that I am struggling with at the present moment, but in His presence alone.

I may not know how to do it well, but I know that I want to fight living in the joy of each day. No matter how terrible we feel, the Lord can still give us joy. Our willingness to choose joy is deeply rooted in our hope and trust in our precious Savior. Let us keep our eyes solely on Him, and it is there that we will find abundant joy for today.

"I want to live in the richness of this day. I look forward to the joy to be found in tomorrow."
-Kara Tippetts[xlii]

joy prayer notes

_____

_____

_____

_____

_____

_____

_____

_____

_____

_____

_____

_____

_____

_____

loneliness

definition: "Affected with, characterized by, or causing a depressing feeling of being alone; lonesome; destitute of sympathetic or friendly companionship, intercourse, support, etc; lone, solitary; without company, companionless."[xliii]

"Turn to me and have mercy, for I am alone and in
deep distress."
-Psalm 25:16-

One of the hardest things for me in the journey with Lyme disease is the severe isolation that it has brought both physically and emotionally. When my health first started to rapidly decline, I had to make the heart-wrenching decision to resign from the job I loved and move out of state to be home with my parents. Like many other Lymies who have been forced to give up their jobs, I was unprepared for the severe isolation that this would bring.

At the time I made the decision I had no idea how sick I was or how long it would be to not only obtain a correct diagnosis, but also to find the right medical team. Throughout the years I have been sadly shocked at this "isolating illness".

I have related well to Job's words in the 19th chapter, verse 14: *"My relatives have failed me, my close friends have forgotten me."* As a person who loves people, the lonely hours upon hours and days upon days spent in bed has been the most difficult part of this journey.

Sadly, like many others in this journey, I have had lots of people leave. Many whom I counted as friends and family have chosen to separate themselves from me and not walk the slow and winding path to healing.

As the minutes and hours piled upon each day, the loneliness sometimes became unbearable. The fear of abandonment and being alone has happened in hundreds of little ways throughout this journey, threatening to overwhelm me if I let it.

In the depths of loneliness my one comfort has been that the Lord has never and will never abandon us. Even on the darkest of days of loneliness, the Lord promises to be close to us and never abandon us. Because of this truth we have the opportunity to learn from this hard and painful lesson.

Loneliness will not just "go away" when we get better and can return to "real life". Learning to have God as our central focus *now* will only help us in the future. There is no person that can "cure" our loneliness. Only God can do that. Unfortunately, I have seen so many Lymics try to rely on others to fill this need of loneliness. What an impossible thing to place on any human- something that God can only fulfill.

As we work through this real pain of loneliness let us have courage to place this real emotion into the hands of the One who loves us more than life. God is always with us, friends, and in that alone we can rest joyfully.

God in His faithfulness, He *always* provides just what we need, not only physically, but emotionally as well. So on the days where loneliness overwhelms us to tears, let us remember that God has promised to be with us always. *"…And remember that I am always with you until the end of time."* (Matthew 28:20, GOD'S WORD Translation)

"The pain of loneliness is one way in which He wants to get our attention. We may be earnestly desiring to be obedient and holy. But we may be missing the fact that it is here, where we happen to be at this moment and not in another place or another time, that we may learn to love Him. Here where it seems He is not at work, where He seems obscure or frightening, where He is not doing what we expected Him to do, where He is most absent. Here and nowhere else is the appointed time. If faith does not go to work here, it will not work at all."
-Elisabeth Elliot-[xliv]

loneliness prayer notes

_____

_____

_____

_____

_____

_____

_____

_____

_____

_____

_____

_____

optimism

definition: "Hopefulness and confidence about the future or the successful outcome of something."[xlv]

"Meanwhile, the moment we get tired in the waiting, God's Spirit is right alongside helping us along. If we don't know how or what to pray, it doesn't matter. He does our praying in and for us, making prayer out of our wordless sighs, our aching groans. He knows us far better than we know ourselves, knows our pregnant condition, and keeps us present before God. That's why we can be so sure that every detail in our lives of love for God is worked into something good."
-Romans 8:26-28, The Message-

Several months ago I had an appointment with a specialist that I had been dreading for weeks. I had already had to delay and reschedule the appointment a couple of times due to some serious situations. The delays had only produced more anxiety in the long run. This appointment, like most all of our appointments as Lymies, included some invasive testing and as the day came closer I struggled deeply with this. This appointment was going to make things more uncomfortable and I was expecting bad news on top of it.

Instead, I was pleasantly and extremely surprised when I found the test was easier than I thought, and I received good news. I walked out of that doctors' appointment completely optimistic about not only the day, but also about the treatment schedule that was before me.

For a little bit of time I used to ride the tidal waves of the emotion of optimism with going up and down. When something good would happen I would be all optimistic that things would go perfectly in the future. When something bad would happen I was convinced that everything would continue to be horrible.

In recent months though I am seeing more clearly the ways that the Lord uses optimism as a gift in this very long journey. As Romans 8:26-28 states, at the exact moment that I feel tired of waiting, the Lord gives a beautiful gift of optimistic hope. It took some time to really search for these moments. At first I wasn't used to looking for them, but now I see them more and more. They are beautiful gifts of optimistic hope from the Lord for today and also for the future.

Friends, today let's search for optimism in this journey. As we do we will be given gifts of optimism to help us along in this very long journey.

"Optimism is the faith that leads to achievement. Nothing can be done without hope and confidence."
-Helen Keller [xlvi]

optimism prayer notes

_____

_____

_____

_____

_____

_____

_____

_____

_____

_____

_____

_____

_____

_____

peace

"Thou wilt keep him in perfect peace whose mind is stayed on thee, because he trusteth in thee."
-Isaiah 26:3-

In this Lyme journey it can be easy to feel anything but peaceful. When I went to write this chapter, I looked up the definition of peace and was surprised to learn that it goes beyond just a state of tranquility and quiet and includes freedom from oppressive thoughts or emotions. I don't know about you, but I often feel overwhelmed with oppressive thoughts about what could possibly be next in this Lyme journey.

Freedom from disquieting or oppressive thoughts seems like something that is completely impossible doesn't it? If I am having a day of pain it can be easy to allow my mind and thoughts to wander and to become frantic that this pain will last forever. If I let it, the sickness threatens to overwhelm me. If I let it, Lyme disease has the potential to rob peace from me.

The verse from Isaiah 26:3 is one that has been a favorite of mine since childhood. I liked it as a child, but in this journey with Lyme disease I have come to know the beautiful wisdom, truth, and depth of this beautiful and profound verse.

A different version of Isaiah 26:3 says, *"You will keep the mind that is dependent on You in perfect peace, for it is trusting in You."* The mind that is dependent on HIM.

Not on the circumstances at hand.

Not on the newest symptom that Lyme decides to throw at us.

Not on the new diagnosis of a new co-infection that is found.

Not on a complication that arises.

Not on the herx that has thrown everything off kilter.

Not on the most recent loved one to walk away.

Not on the newest cure that we may see shared on social media.

Not on the doctor who says that we will never get better.

Not on *any* of that, friends.

The mind that stays on God is the one at peace.

Keeping our minds dependent on Him is the only way we can bring peace in this journey no matter what else is going on with this disease. Dear friends, keep your mind on Him. Meditate on Scripture. Read it over and over and over again. Memorize it if you can. Can't memorize a whole chapter? Work on a verse. Can't memorize a verse? Work on a word.

Saturate your mind with HIS truth today and everyday and He will bless you with His peace all of the days of this journey. *"The LORD gives His people strength. The LORD blesses them with peace."* (Psalm 29:11)

"If God be our God, He will give us peace in trouble. When there is a storm without, He will make peace within. The world can create trouble in peace, but God can create peace in trouble."
-Thomas Watson-[xlviii]

peace prayer notes

---

pity

definition: "Sympathetic or kindly sorrow evoked by the suffering, distress, or misfortune of another; to feel pity or compassion for; be sorry for; commiserate with."[xlix]

"He feels pity for the weak and the needy, and He will rescue them."
-Psalm 72:13-

It had been a whirlwind of 10 days as I had flown across the country to meet with my main medical team, test dosed several new medications (which is always an adventure with my fragile system) and faced one of my biggest fears in this journey: having a port catheter placed. Two days after surgery, I found myself back in the treatment room, to have my port accessed for the first time.

As the nurse came at me with the largest needle I had ever seen, I asked (only half-jokingly) *"and where are you putting that?"*. My kind nurse gave me a look of pity and explained the process of having a port accessed. I was in shock as the sting of the access needle being inserted into my tender surgical area was tampered with. Tears filled my eyes and all of a sudden my exhausted body felt completely overwhelmed by the thought of being accessed regularly for treatment. My compassionate nurse saw the look on my face, took pity on me, touched my arm and kindly encouraged me saying; *"Take one day at a time, Rebecca. You can do this."*

She stepped back to throw away the trash and I took a few deep breaths as I glanced around the room. I was met with looks of compassion from others until my gaze rested on a young woman who was nervously sitting on the edge of a chair, clutching her purse in front of her, her eyes wildly moving darting between patients, IV poles, and the nurses. I knew immediately that it was her first time in the room and my heart broke for her.

My kind-hearted nurse approached the young woman talking encouragingly to her as she glanced at the doctors' orders. The woman quickly looked around at all of us in the treatment room and loudly stated, *"I am not here for anything but blood work. I don't need anything else like an IV."* My nurse calmly completed the doctors' orders and in a matter of 30 seconds had taken the required vial of blood. As the nurse prepared to put a band aid on the woman, we all started as the woman jumped up and screamed that she had just endured the worst experience of her life and that she would never do blood work again. Looking around, she quickly rushed out of the room.

It was quiet in the treatment room as my tear-filled eyes met the looks of the others. We all had the same look- pity. Pity for this young woman at the start of this journey, of what we knew was to come, and of what we all were experiencing. I looked around and saw the veteran looks of people who had been through a war and were fighting for their lives and wept once more.

I have been the recipient of pity many times

throughout this part of my story from those who love and know me well and from strangers alike. In this I have been met with deep compassion and am challenged to meet others in their stories with the same compassion and pity.

Pity that evokes emotion that causes me to see others and their sorrows gives me the opportunity to spread the kindness of the Lord in new ways to those who are hurting and broken-hearted. Pity that inspires me to have a gentle heart to see the world in a new way that will change the course of each Lyme patient I encounter. In our pain, in our weakness, and in our need, Jesus will meet us, and we can pass this grace and Godly pity onto each person we encounter.

"Do not scorn pity that is the gift of a gentle heart..."
-J.R.R. Tolkien[1]

pity prayer notes

_____

_____

_____

_____

_____

_____

_____

_____

_____

_____

_____

_____

_____

_____

_____

rejection

definition: "to refuse to accept (someone or something); rebuff; to discard as useless or unsatisfactory."[viii]

"Therefore, as God's chosen people, holy and dearly loved, clothe yourselves with compassion, kindness, humility, gentleness, and patience."
-Colossians 3:12-

Several weeks ago I went in for a routine ultrasound and came out in tears after hearing that I needed an unexpected surgery. There was a good possibility that I was looking at Ovarian Cancer. Having recently lost several people I knew to Ovarian Cancer I was near hysteria. I quickly texted several of my closest friends and asked for prayers. I heard back immediately from all but one. Over the next few weeks I heard from this friend less than a handful of times until she went completely silent. I tried reaching out, but there was no response. Over the weeks I realized the silence shouted louder than any words that may have been said. I had been rejected.

It had happened before in this journey, being abandoned by friends, but this rejection hit me differently. Typically in this journey rejection happened when I was told that I didn't have enough faith to be healed, or that a friend was tired of walking the long road of Lyme. This was different in that the silence seemed to confirm what others had said. Due to social media I was able to see that this friend's life went happily on while I had been left behind, bruised and hurt behind the scenes.

I felt more vulnerable than ever and wept at being left alone, not worthy of love and friendship because of this disease and the complications that come with it.

Rejection does this to us doesn't it? It makes you feel that you are not worthy of the love and life that God has for us.

Lyme in its uniqueness emphasizes this. From the well-known doctors who say that Lyme doesn't exist, to family and loved ones who walk away during this journey. We are constantly rejected by the medical community, by doctors, by the government and finally when rejection hits home to those closest to us the rejection can feel particularly wounding.

How do we handle this? If we allow our hearts to become bitter from rejection, then we fill our hearts with darkness rather than God's love. Rejection hurts there is no doubt about it, but as we bring our brokenness to the Lord we are met with all of the love we could have ever wanted. *"The LORD is close to the brokenhearted; He rescues those whose spirits are crushed."* (Psalm 34:18) The Lord truly will rescue our broken and rejected spirits. Hold fast to Him friends.

"Rejection steals the best of who I am by reinforcing the worst of what's been said to me."
-Lysa Terkeurst[liii]

rejection prayer notes

_____

_____

_____

_____

_____

_____

_____

_____

_____

_____

_____

_____

_____

sadness

"You are now very sad. But later I will see you, and you will be so happy that no one will be able to change the way you feel."
-John 16:22-

There are certain days in this journey where sadness can threaten to overwhelm our hearts. For me, this often happens around certain times of the year. It causes me to stop and think more reflectively on what I feel that this disease has "stolen from me" and how it has changed and affected my life.

One of these times of sadness is at the beginning of a new school year. Having been a former high school teacher and loving my job, it has been extremely painful not teaching these last four years. Before I got sick, my life in so many ways revolved around the school year. The excitement of being in the classroom and feeling like I was making a difference gave me purpose.

I remember approaching the new school year the first year I was home with a false bravado. I counted down the days on the calendar and sent former co-workers gift cards to coffee places along with heartfelt notes and prayers for their new year. Behind the scenes, I cried myself to sleep every night as the days got closer to seeing school buses come around the neighborhood.

Finally, a couple of weeks before the new year I insisted on going to Target to pick up a few medical supplies. I was struggling to walk at that point and, yet I headed off.

As I hobbled through the doors, I was immediately hit with all of the school year signs and supplies. I stood at the "Target dollar spot" with tears running down my face as I watched moms and dads help their children pick out new items for the year. I stood and watched as two young women talked excitedly about the things they were finding that would help them decorate their classrooms on their limited budgets. I stood for a good ten minutes with people passing me on all sides, until I finally turned and limped out of the store, physically and emotionally sad. It took me close to ten minutes to get to my car, and when I collapsed in the front seat, I wept. I wept at the time of year, but mostly I wept at my sadness for experiencing all that I had lost.

I personally believe that sadness in this Lyme disease journey is a realistic component. We must face so many difficult things and it is easy to become sad at the state of where we find ourselves. Our lives often look completely different than they looked before, and it can be tempting to dwell in the sadness of this fact.

I came across John 16:22 this past year. It has been a verse that I have been working on memorizing and focusing on in times of sadness in this journey. While we may be very sad now, the Lord promises a future of happiness where no one will be able to change how we feel. This promise may be true for our earthly lives, but we can rest confidently assured that it is definitely true for our heavenly lives.

Dear friends, on the days of sadness where you find yourselves crying and weeping with no reprieve, hold on to hope. Our weeping ends as we put our hope in a future life without sadness.

"Shining is always costly. We are apt to feel that we are doing the greatest good in the world when we are strong, and able for active duty, and when the heart and hands are full of kindly service. When we are called aside and can only suffer; when we are sick; when we are consumed with pain; when all of our activities have been dropped, we feel that we are no longer of use, that we are not doing anything. But if we are patient and submissive, it is almost certain that we are a greater blessing to the world in our time of suffering and pain than we were in the days when we thought we were doing the most of our work. We are burning now, and shining because we are burning. Never forget the glory of tomorrow is rooted in the drudgery of today."
-Streams in the Desert[lv]

sadness prayer notes

_____

_____

_____

_____

_____

_____

_____

_____

_____

_____

_____

_____

_____

shame

definition: "A painful emotion caused by consciousness of guilt, shortcoming; a condition of humiliating disgrace."[xvi]

"Fear not, for you will not be put to shame; and do not feel humiliated for you will not be disgraced."
-Isaiah 54:4-

Shame, I was to find, was to be a strange accompanying emotion in this journey. Overtime it has lessened, but in the beginning of this journey it definitely threatened to overwhelm me. Questions (that I am sure were intended to be kind and caring) only intensified this feeling. In many ways, even though I was extremely lonely, I was grateful for the distance from some friends and the lack of communication. I felt ashamed of the story that God was writing. Every time someone would ask me what I did, I would think, *"I don't know. I don't recognize myself or anything anymore."* I often wondered how to introduce myself.

For so many years, I used to introduce myself with ease as I quickly followed up the question to "what do you do?" with lots of answers. In these last years I have learned the painful truth that many people do not have an answer that can be given in five seconds flat. We strive to define ourselves by our careers, our marriages, or our children. Then when illness strikes we start to have shame that the story that is being written is one of illness. Our ultimate definition cannot come from any of these things, because our worth and definition should solely be found in the Lord, whether we are sick or not.

Several years ago I returned to Washington DC where I had lived for some time, to attend a dear friend's wedding. A few minutes before the wedding was to start I ran into a former student. I was coming off of a fun-filled, yet very busy days of hanging out with friends. To be frank, I was pretty exhausted. My former student kindly asked how I was doing and how life was. After a few minutes of giving general answers, he proceeded to ask if I was still teaching, to which I replied "I am not sure if you heard, but I'm sick." He was completely taken back at my abruptness and to be honest so was I. As he stuttered to ask if I was okay, I gave a quick spiel about Lyme and its co-infections.

After a few minutes we parted ways, and I realized belatedly that I had been trying to justify what I perceive was my story. I was ashamed. My shame revolves around where I long to live, but am not. My shame is rooted in the story I long to have, instead of the one I do have. A story that I believe would be much better than a story of Lyme disease and its co-infections could ever be. A story that is a based on a life filled with doing more for the Lord than I am physically able to do.

Shame is a strange beast, isn't it? It makes us feel that we are not enough. That the story the Lord is writing which includes Lyme disease is one that needs to have an apology and an explanation. That the story is less than the one without Lyme. Shame has the ability to convince us that our stories with Lyme are something to feel humiliated over.

Friends, it is simply not true. Shame is *not* the story being written. Your beautiful life and purpose are what is being written. Let us re-write the feel of shame with the beautiful truth from the Lord. "*Those who look to Him are radiant; their faces are never covered with shame.*" (Psalm 34:5)

"*I wasn't full of shame because of some huge sin in my past; I was full of shame because somewhere along the road, I decided that my definition of myself was more accurate than God's definition of me.*"
-Blythe Hunt-[lvii]

shame prayer notes

_____

_____

_____

_____

_____

_____

_____

_____

_____

_____

_____

_____

_____

_____

terror

definition: "Intense, sharp, overmastering fear; an instance or cause of intense fear or anxiety."[lviii]

"Do not be afraid of sudden terror..."
-Proverbs 3:25-

In the early morning hours of May 1st, 2015, I was awakened feeling incredibly sick, yet unable to move due to severe vertigo and dizziness. Even though I was laying down with my eyes closed, the room wouldn't stop spinning. I quickly tried to use my cell phone to call my parents who were sound asleep across the hallway. It took more than twenty minutes to be able to see the phone clearly enough to dial the numbers.

The room was completely dark and I was absolutely terrified. As my mom sat with me for the next hour, she continuously prayed for help, and I wept as I just kept whispering, "Jesus, Jesus, Jesus. Please help. Jesus. Help." After a couple of hours the vertigo and dizziness had subsided a brief amount to where I sent my mom back to bed. Alone, I laid in the dark for hours terrified and hoping that the morning light would bring a change.

Unfortunately it didn't.

Twenty-six long and terrifying days later I was finally able to leave my house briefly for the first time. Nine days after that I weakly and tentatively flew out to my doctors' office across the country to start a new intensive treatment for beating this horrible disease.

It will be two years since this happened, and yet even writing about this situation causes a feeling of terror and panic deep within my soul, as I remember those incredibly long days. For those long and lonely thirty-seven days, I lived in a constant state of terror.

First, I wondered if I would ever be able to get out of bed without severe vertigo again. Second, I grew to fear that I would be forced to live with this unwelcome symptom for the rest of my life. Third, I was terrified that if I did get better it would happen again.

For the first couple of weeks, I lived mostly in the dark and I was unable to watch TV, read books, or listen to music as any stimulation was too much for my fragile body. Terrified, I wept constantly and feared the present and the future. As the weeks progressed and I watched the calendar days slowly slip by, I lived in terror of what else would happen and if this would strike again. As I slowly healed from what we believe was an intense reaction to a new herb, I silently wondered if there was another cause that we weren't seeing. For months, I was terrified to go to sleep, afraid that the same thing would happen. For nearly a year, I would feel a deep panic anytime I felt the least bit dizzy.

Terror happens in this Lyme disease journey. Usually it happens without a moment's notice and strikes the deepest fear in our hearts and souls. Since that dark night in May 2015, I have had other times of terror.

Another terror is the monster of what could happen that we must fight. When these feelings of terror threaten to overwhelm me I cling to the beautiful promise from Psalm 91:5: *"You do not need to fear terrors of the night, arrows that fly during the day."* (GOD'S WORD Translation)

"Tell those who are terrified, be brave and don't be afraid. Your God will come… He will come and rescue you."
-Isaiah 35:4, GOD'S WORD Translation[lix]

terror prayer notes

_____

_____

_____

_____

_____

_____

_____

_____

_____

_____

_____

_____

_____

_____

weariness

definition: "Physically or mentally exhausted by hard work, exertion, strain, etc; fatigued; tired; characterized by or causing impatience or dissatisfaction; tedious…"[ix]

"Come to me, all you who are weary and burdened, and I will give you rest."
-Matthew 11:28-

Before I got sick, I remember staying up every night, studying for my second masters, holding a full-time teaching job, and grading papers late into the night. I tried to balance everything that was on my plate and live a healthy life.

There are times that we all try and balance everything, yet end up sleep deprived and exhausted. Often times the rush of life and demands that we put on ourselves overrun us. Exhaustion, weariness, and tiredness – everyone experiences it, but with Lyme we experience a different weariness, don't we? A weariness that is hard to explain to those outside this journey.

It is hard to even put into words to those who don't know and understand Lyme with all the different requirements. There are so many different treatments, alternative therapies, detox solutions, supplements, etc. It can all become so tiring. One day recently I said to my mom, *"I am so tired, a deep tiredness and in reality mom, I am weary of this fight."*

In this situation the weariness won't be staved off or

helped by green tea or coffee. Instead, we come to realize that our weariness can only be cured by giving this to the Lord. The verse from Matthew 11:28 truly speaks to my heart about pressing forward into the Lord and taking our weariness to Him.

Another verse that has really spoken to my weariness throughout this journey is from Galatians 6:9. It states, *"Let us not become weary in doing good, for at the proper time we will reap a harvest if we do not give up."* This verse speaks to weariness and encourages us to continue as we will reap a harvest of blessing, if we don't give up.

I used to think that I would arrive at the end of this journey quickly. I hoped and prayed that I would arrive gracefully and come out a more mature person. Instead, Lyme disease has taught me that there will always be times of weariness in life. It doesn't just end when we arrive at the end of Lyme. Instead, Lyme has become a beautiful teaching ground for changing me. Gently, compassionately, and graciously the Lord has gently matured me.

Today as I feel wearier then ever and I embark on another new treatment option and session, I remember this: I commit to the Lord my weariness. He promises that as I come to Him, that He will give rest. No matter how I feel, I can trust that as I press forward, leaning on the Lord, He will guide, refresh, and bring a harvest of blessings.

No matter how long this fight lasts, we can overcome weariness with the Lord's help. We can rest assured that the Lord will meet us in our deepest weariness of moments to breathe life into us as He gives us rest. Hold on, dear friends, keep pushing forward, keep trusting, and keep taking each weary day to the Lord.

He will meet us. He will be our rest.

"I will go anywhere and do anything in order to communicate the love of Jesus to those who do not know Him or have forgotten Him."
-St. Frances Cabrini-[lxi]

weariness prayer notes

---

a note from rebecca

Sweet Friend,

My prayer in writing this book is what I stated in the introduction- that it will be a gentle reminder that in the vast myriad of emotions of Lyme disease the Lord is near and understands. I hope and pray that this book will be what you need to walk through this hard season and be a help and encouragement throughout the changing emotions that accompany this journey.

For some of you, dear friends, this book may only serve as a starting place and you may want more. I am not a licensed counselor, and this book does not take the place of therapy. There are wonderful licensed Christian counselors who would love to come along side you as you navigate these emotions should you want to talk through and work through these emotions more. Please, if this is you, my heart prays that you will have the courage to look and search for counseling help. I pray that in this journey that you will find a committed Christian counselor who can walk through the physical and the spiritual dimensions of emotions that accompany this journey.

You are not alone.
You are not forgotten.
You are truly seen.

I'm praying for you, dear friend, and I trust you'll be praying for me as well as continue to fight the good fight and walk this journey before us.

With Love, Rebecca

index list of scripture references & versions

DESPAIR
Isaiah 9:1- New Living Translation
2 Corinthians 1:8- New International Version
Isaiah 8:21-22- New International Version

DISGUST
Psalm 119:158- English Standard Version

DISTRACTION
Mark 14:32, 37-40- New Living Translation
Isaiah 60:1-2- New International Version
Romans 15:13- New Living Translation
Isaiah 42:16- New International Version
Hosea 6:3- New Living Translation

FEAR
Psalm 3:5-6- The Message
Psalm 3:8- New International Version
Psalm 18:28-New Living Translation
Psalm 56:3- New International Version

FRUSTRATION
Galatians 6:9- New Living Translation

GRIEF
Isaiah 53:4- English Standard Version
Psalm 9:18- New Living Translation
Psalm 31:14-15- New Living Translation

GUILT
I Peter 4:16- English Standard Version
Hebrews 12:1- New Living Translation

HOPE
Psalm 130:7- New Living Translation
Psalm 6:6-7- New International Version
Psalm 6:3- New International Version
Psalm 31:24- New Living Translation
Psalm 33:20-21- New International Version
Psalm 33:22- New Living Translation

HOPELESSNESS
Psalm 34:18- Good News Translation
Psalm 10:17- New Living Translation
Hosea 2:15- New International Version
Job 13:15- King James Version

JEALOUSY
Psalm 73:4- New Living Translation
Psalm 73:5- New International Version
Psalm 85:12- New Living Translation
Proverbs 14:30- New Living Translation

JOY
Psalm 16:11- Holman Christian Standard Bible

LONELINESS
Psalm 25:16- New Living Translation
Job 19:14- English Standard Version
Matthew 28:20- GOD'S WORD Translation

OPTIMISM
Romans 8:26-28- The Message

PEACE
Isaiah 26:3- King James Version
Isaiah 26:3- Holman Christian Standard Bible
Psalm 29:11- New Living Translation

PITY
Psalm 72:13- New Living Translation

REJECTION
Colossians 3:12- New International Version
Psalm 34:18- New Living Translation

SADNESS
John 16:22- Contemporary English Version

SHAME
Isaiah 54:4- New American Standard Bible
Psalm 34:5- New International Version

TERROR
Proverbs 3:25- English Standard Version
Psalm 91:5- GOD'S WORD Translation

WEARINESS
Matthew 11:28- New International Version
Galatians 6:9- New Living Translation

about the author

Rebecca VanDeMark is a writer, speaker, and blogger who loves Jesus, life, and the miracle of hope. Rebecca is the author of five books, including, *"Praying through Lyme Disease"*. Rebecca holds degrees from Cedarville University, Regent University, and American University. Before fighting health issues Rebecca worked in Washington DC with two non-profit organizations and later taught High School History and Bible Classes for seven years. Rebecca loves celebrating the beauty of the ordinary each day as she fights Lyme disease in addition to other health issues. She lives with her family, splitting time between the sweet south and upstate New York.

Connect with Rebecca on a daily basis, see pictures, and follow her writing and speaking ministry:

Website: www.rebeccavandemark.com
Blog: www.caravansonnet.com
Instagram:
www.instagram.com/rebeccaannvandemark
Facebook:
www.facebook.com/rebeccaannvandemark
Twitter:
www.twitter.com/caravansonnet
Email:
rebeccaannvandemark@gmail.com

---

[i] Tripp, Paul David.
https://www.goodreads.com/quotes/432604-every-day-you-preach-to-yourself-a-gospel-of-your
[ii] http://www.thefreedictionary.com/acceptance
[iii] http://www.biblestudytools.com/dictionary/content-contentment/
[iv]http://www.elisabethelliot.org/ramble/ramblings070310.html
[v] http://www.dictionary.com/browse/anger
[vi] http://www.merriam-webster.com/dictionary/rage
[vii] Angelou, Maya.
https://www.goodreads.com/quotes/41814-bitterness-is-like-cancer-it-eats-upon-the-host-but
http://www.mundanefaithfulness.com/2014/12/29/by-degrees-living-and-dying/
[viii] http://www.dictionary.com/browse/apprehension
[ix] Psalm 112:7, New Living Translation.
[x] http://www.merriam-webster.com/dictionary/anticipation
[xi] *Great is Thy Faithfulness.* [Words: Thomas Chisholm, 1923. Music and arrangement: William M. Runyan, 1923.]
[xii] http://www.dictionary.com/browse/bored
[xiii] www.cbsnews.com/news/christopher-lane-australian-baseball-player-killed-by-bored-okla-teens-police-say
[xiv]http://www.christianstudylibrary.org/files/pub/articles/20150080%20-%20Alderson%20D%20-%20The%20Wisdom%20of%20Martyn%20Lloyd-Jones.pdf
[xv] Pope Francis.
https://twitter.com/pontifex/status/351286563709263876?lang=en Tweet- June 30, 2013.
[xvi] http://www.merriam-webster.com/dictionary/courage
[xvii] Deuteronomy 31:6-8, New International Version.
[xviii] Tripp, Paul. *New Morning Mercies: A Daily Gospel Devotional.* (Wheaton, Illinois: Crossway Publishing, 2014.)

xix http://www.dictionary.com/browse/despair
xx https://www.youtube.com/watch?v=NKEPRICkQDs
xxi https://www.youtube.com/watch?v=NKEPRICkQDs
xxii http://www.whatchristianswanttoknow.com/25-awesome-perseverance-quotes/
xxiii http://www.merriam-webster.com/dictionary/disgust
xxiv Rohn, Jim. https://twitter.com/officialjimrohn/status/755470110937284609
xxv http://www.merriam-webster.com/dictionary/distraction
xxvi Moore, Beth. https://www.pinterest.com/pin/75013150017498730/
xxvii http://www.dictionary.com/browse/fear
xxviii *Your Great Name.* [Words: Michael Neele and Krissy Nordhoff. Music and arrangement: Natalie Grant, 2010.]
xxix https://en.oxforddictionaries.com/definition/frustration
xxx Unknown. Quote found on Pinterest with no source.
xxxi http://www.medicinenet.com/script/main/art.asp?articlekey=24274
xxxii https://twitter.com/johnpiper/status/704653441533132800
xxxiii http://www2.merriam-webster.com/cgi-bin/mwdictsn?book=Dictionary&va=guilt
xxxiv http://www.goodreads.com/quotes/26397 guilt-is-a-rope-that-wears-thin
xxxv http://www.dictionary.com/browse/hope
xxxvi Strobel, Lee. *The Case for Hope: Looking Ahead with Confidence and Courage.* (Grand Rapids, Michigan: Zondervan Publishing, 2015.)
xxxvii http://www.dictionary.com/browse/hopelessness
xxxviii Elliot, Elisabeth. http://www.elisabethelliot.org/newsletters/2003-01-02.pdf .
xxxix http://www.dictionary.com/browse/jealous
xl VanDeMark, Rebecca. *September Caravan.* (New York:

Richard Weiskotten Publishing, 2017.)

[xli] http://www.merriam-webster.com/dictionary/joy

[xlii] Tippetts, Kara. Mundane Faithfulness Blog. *"The Dream"*. Originally posted: October 3, 2015. Reposted: April 7, 2016. http://acacia.pair.com/Acacia.Vignettes/Day.By.Day.html

[xliii] http://www.dictionary.com/browse/loneliness

[xliv] Elliot, Elizabeth. *The Path of Loneliness: Finding Your Way through the Wilderness to God.* (Ann Arbor, MI: Servant Publications, 1988 & 2001.)

[xlv] https://www.google.com/#q=definition+of+optimism

[xlvi] https://www.brainyquote.com/quotes/quotes/h/helen kelle164579.html?src=t_optimism

[xlvii] http://www.merriam-webster.com/dictionary/peace

[xlviii] *Watson, Thomas.* Quote found on Internet, this specific website had lots of other encouraging quotes on Christian peace. https://www.christianquotes.info/top-quotes/19-beautiful-quotes-about-gods-peace/#axzz4cqWYkORU

[xlix] http://www.dictionary.com/browse/pity

[l] Tolkien, J.R.R. https://www.goodreads.com/quotes/547296-do-not-scorn-pity-that-is-the-gift-of-a

[li] http://www.dictionary.com/browse/reject

[lii] See also: https://www.vocabulary.com/dictionary/rejection

[liii] Terkeurst, Lysa. Uninvited: Living Loved When You Feel Less Than, Left Out, and Lonely. (Nashville: Tomas Nelson Publications, 2016) page 9.

[liv] http://www.thefreedictionary.com/sadness

[lv] Streams in the Desert. http://www.youdevotion.com/streams/april/26

[lvi] http://www.merriam-webster.com/dictionary/shame

[lvii] Hunt, Blythe. Mundane Faithfulness Blog. *"Living Unashamed"*. Posted- February 24, 2017. http://www.mundanefaithfulness.com/home/2017/2/24/living-unashamed

[lviii] http://www.dictionary.com/browse/terror
[lix] Isaiah 35:4, GOD'S WORD Translation.
[lx] http://www.dictionary.com/browse/weariness
[lxi] St. Francis Cabrini.
http://www.caravansonnet.com/2016/04/mother-cabrini-shrine-peru-new-york.html

coming november 2017

WHEN LYME INVADES
RELEASING NOVEMBER 1ST, 2017

WHEN LYME

INVADES

ENCOURAGEMENT AND PRACTICAL TIPS FOR LOVING YOUR FRIEND THROUGH LYME DISEASE

REBECCA VANDEMARK
AUTHOR OF PRAYING THROUGH LYME DISEASE

also available from Rebecca

PRAYING THROUGH LYME DISEASE
2ND EDITION RELEASING JUNE 2017
LARGE PRINT EDITION RELEASING JUNE
2017

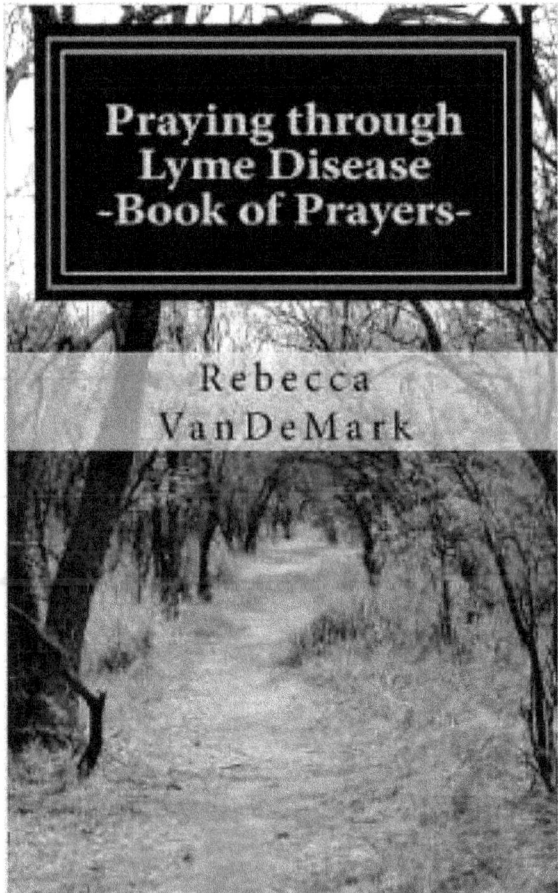

also available from Rebecca
WHEN LIGHT DAWNS
LARGE PRINT EDITION RELEASING
NOVEMBER 2018

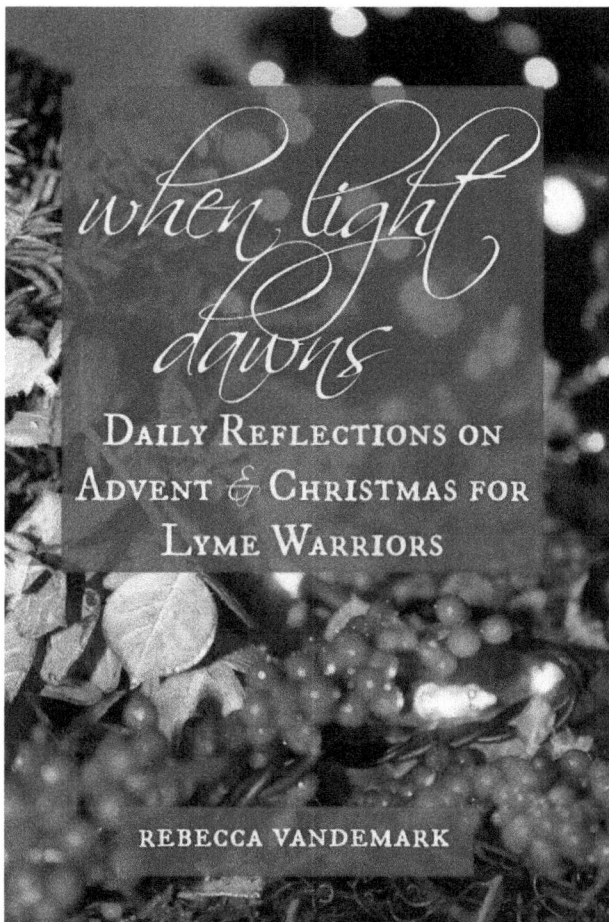

112

also available from Rebecca
PATH OF HOPE
LARGE PRINT EDITION RELEASING JULY
2017

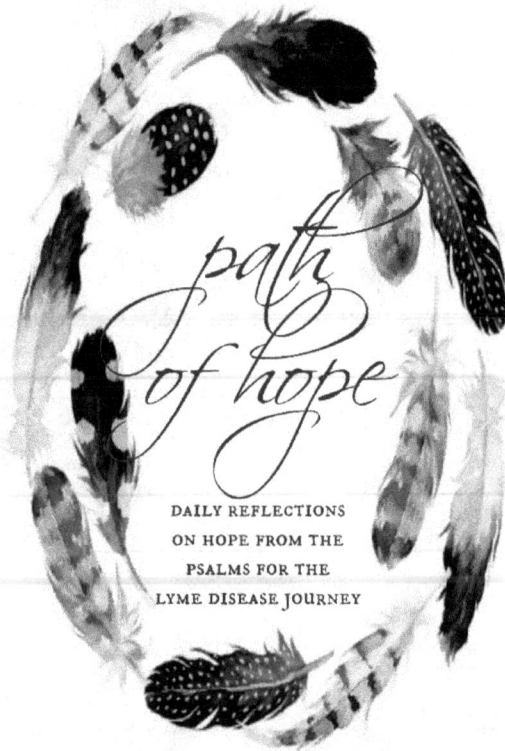

DAILY REFLECTIONS
ON HOPE FROM THE
PSALMS FOR THE
LYME DISEASE JOURNEY

REBECCA VANDEMARK
author of Praying Through Lyme Disease